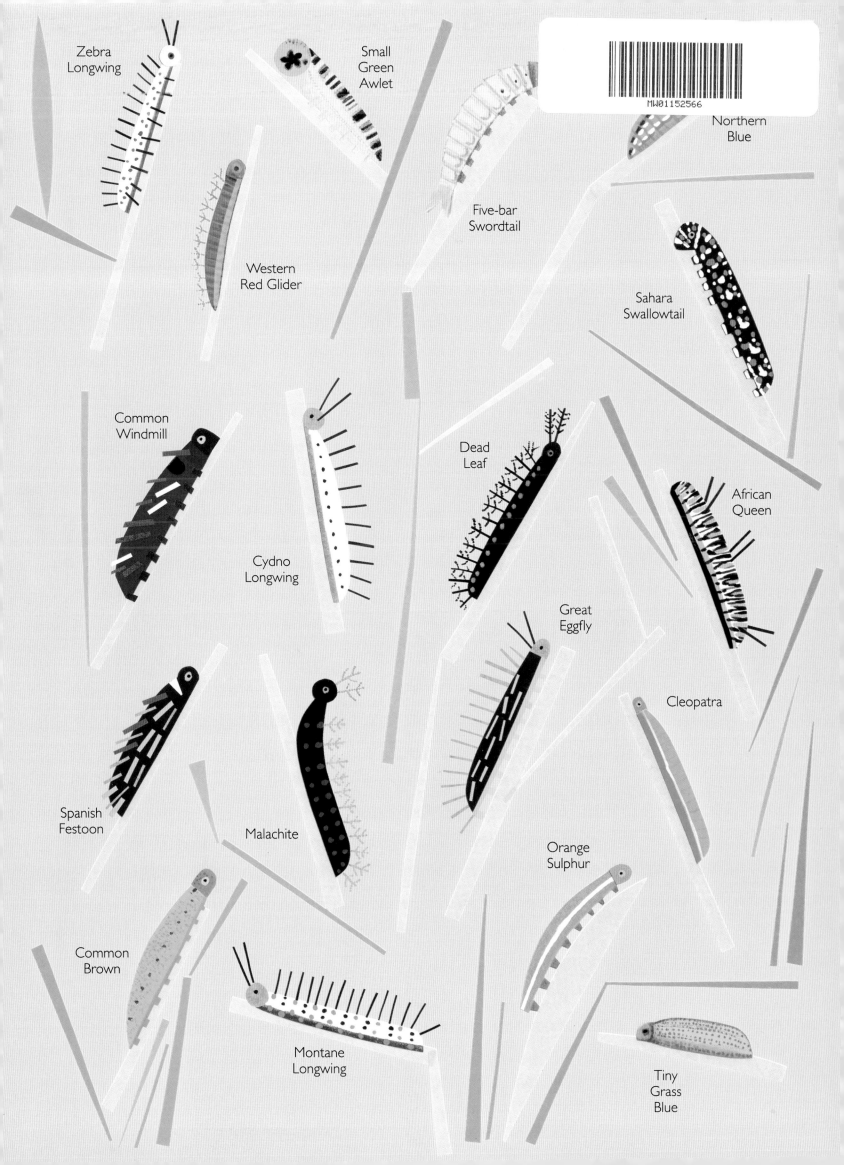

Zebra Longwing

Small Green Awlet

Northern Blue

Five-bar Swordtail

Western Red Glider

Sahara Swallowtail

Common Windmill

Dead Leaf

African Queen

Cydno Longwing

Great Eggfly

Cleopatra

Spanish Festoon

Malachite

Orange Sulphur

Common Brown

Montane Longwing

Tiny Grass Blue

Max,

You're probably wondering why we got you a butterfly book. I'm not sure either. My guess: butterflies are pretty. And free... they flutter wherever they please. And probably because there's a metaphor for life... just like a ~~butterfly~~ caterpillar, you can change. We just hope you don't live in a chrysalis. PS, they used to call a chrysalis a "cocoon."

Anyway, be the butterfly! We love you so much!

Jason & Morgan♡
11/4/22

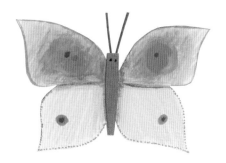

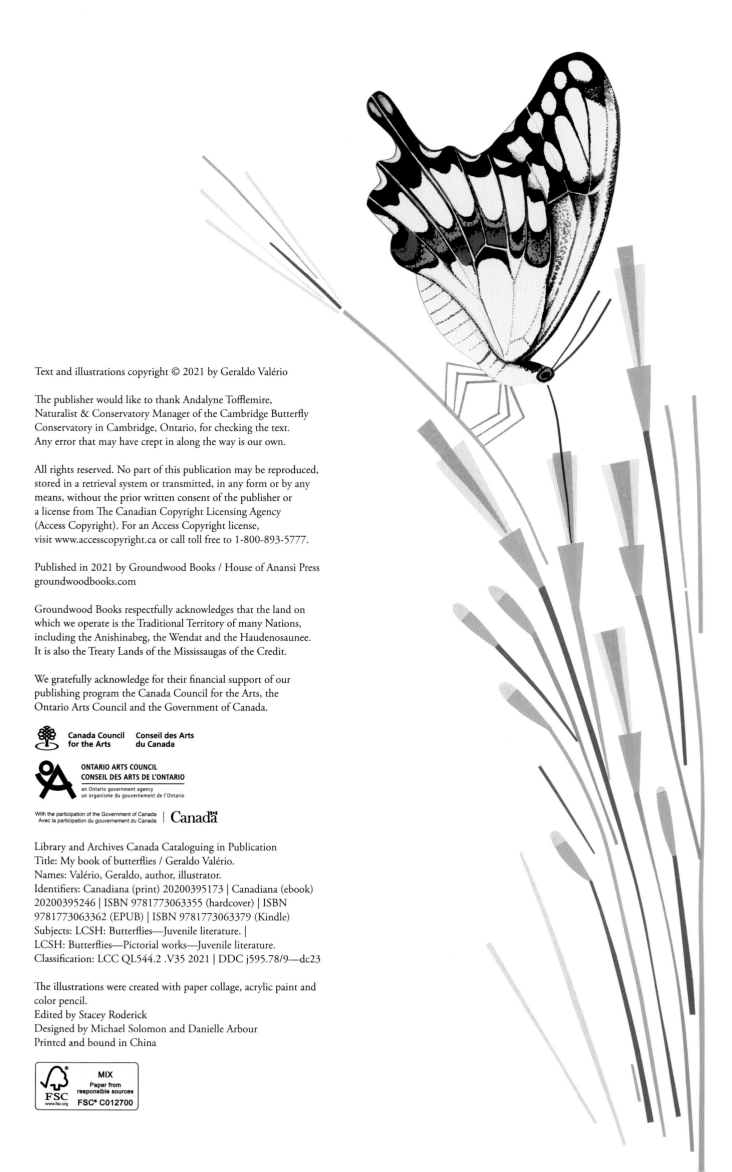

The publisher would like to thank Andalyne Tofflemire,
Naturalist & Conservatory Manager of the Cambridge Butterfly
Conservatory in Cambridge, Ontario, for checking the text.
Any error that may have crept in along the way is our own.

Published in 2021 by Groundwood Books / House of Anansi Press
groundwoodbooks.com

Groundwood Books respectfully acknowledges that the land on
which we operate is the Traditional Territory of many Nations,
including the Anishinabeg, the Wendat and the Haudenosaunee.
It is also the Treaty Lands of the Mississaugas of the Credit.

We gratefully acknowledge for their financial support of our
publishing program the Canada Council for the Arts, the
Ontario Arts Council and the Government of Canada.

Canada Council   Conseil des Arts
for the Arts   du Canada

ONTARIO ARTS COUNCIL
CONSEIL DES ARTS DE L'ONTARIO
an Ontario government agency
un organisme du gouvernement de l'Ontario

With the participation of the Government of Canada   Canadä
Avec la participation du gouvernement du Canada

Library and Archives Canada Cataloguing in Publication
Title: My book of butterflies / Geraldo Valério.
Names: Valério, Geraldo, author, illustrator.
Identifiers: Canadiana (print) 20200395173 | Canadiana (ebook)
20200395246 | ISBN 9781773063355 (hardcover) | ISBN
9781773063362 (EPUB) | ISBN 9781773063379 (Kindle)
Subjects: LCSH: Butterflies—Juvenile literature. |
LCSH: Butterflies—Pictorial works—Juvenile literature.
Classification: LCC QL544.2 .V35 2021 | DDC j595.78/9—dc23

The illustrations were created with paper collage, acrylic paint and
color pencil.
Edited by Stacey Roderick
Designed by Michael Solomon and Danielle Arbour
Printed and bound in China

MY
BOOK *of*
BUTTERFLIES

GERALDO VALÉRIO

GROUNDWOOD BOOKS   HOUSE OF ANANSI PRESS   TORONTO / BERKELEY

INTRODUCTION

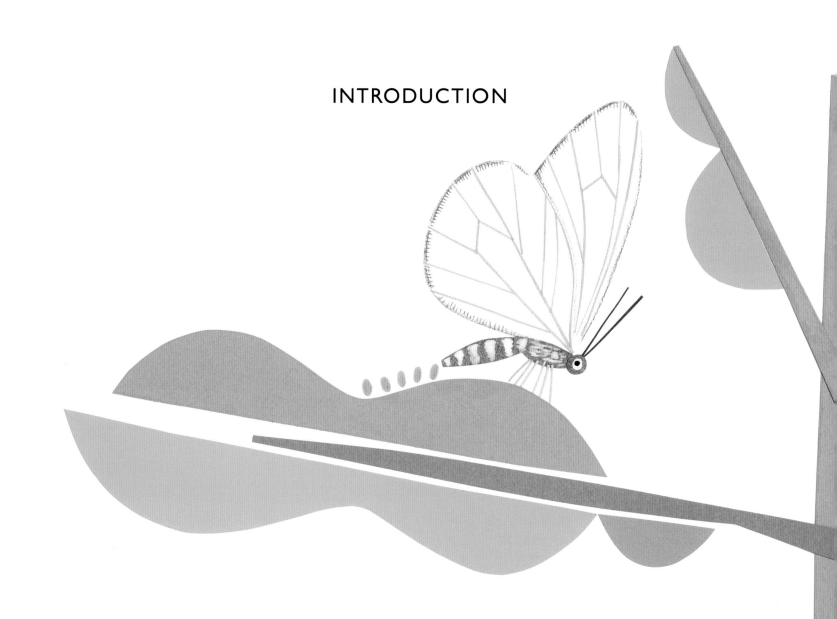

When I was a child in Brazil, my family had a vegetable garden in the backyard of our house. The garden had many different animal visitors — frogs, birds, beetles and spiders.

But I have never forgotten the white butterflies that also visited the vegetable patch. They would flutter around the collard greens, leaving behind their tiny yellow eggs. After a few days, the little eggs turned into hungry caterpillars. Then when the caterpillars grew big enough, they would go to sleep inside their chrysalides. I always wanted to see that magical moment when a butterfly emerged from its chrysalis, but I never got the chance.

As I grew up, I learned about many more unique and beautiful butterflies. There is one as large as a dinner plate and another as small as a dime. Some have coloring that helps them hide, while others have markings that scare away predators.

This book is a collection of my creative impressions of different butterflies from around the world. The layering of these paper collages reminded me of the scales in butterfly wings. I used my imagination to make them, and I hope your imagination will also take flight as you learn about these beautiful creatures.

METAMORPHOSIS: A BUTTERFLY'S LIFE CYCLE

All butterflies begin life as a tiny egg. As they grow and mature, they go through a number of changes.

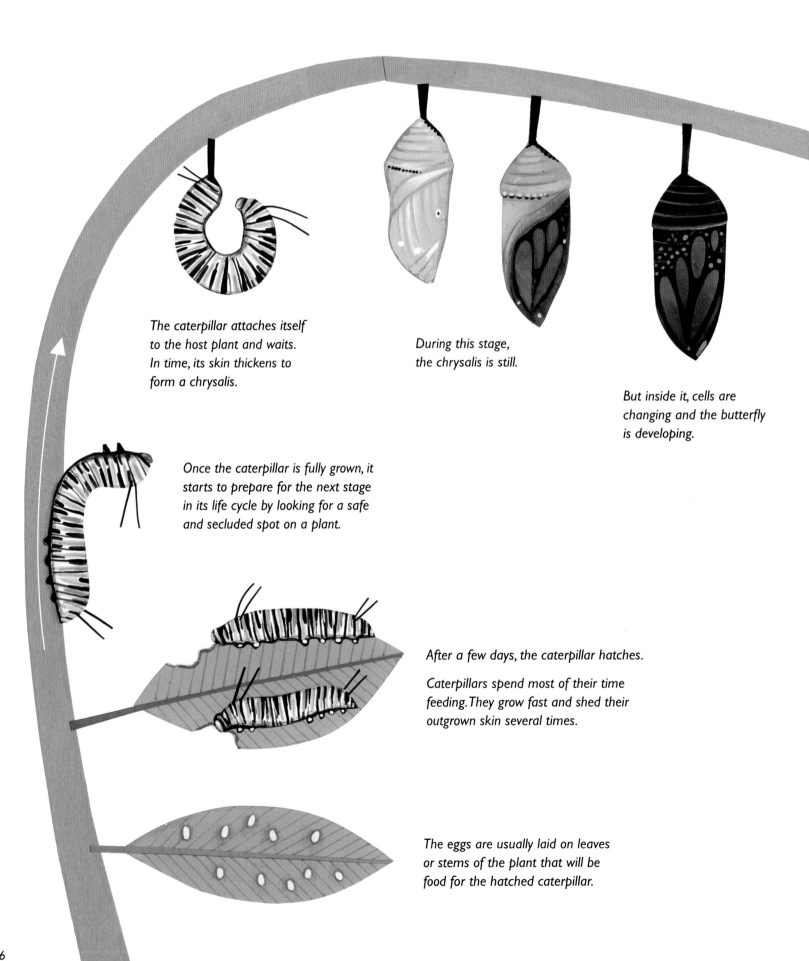

The caterpillar attaches itself to the host plant and waits. In time, its skin thickens to form a chrysalis.

During this stage, the chrysalis is still.

But inside it, cells are changing and the butterfly is developing.

Once the caterpillar is fully grown, it starts to prepare for the next stage in its life cycle by looking for a safe and secluded spot on a plant.

After a few days, the caterpillar hatches.

Caterpillars spend most of their time feeding. They grow fast and shed their outgrown skin several times.

The eggs are usually laid on leaves or stems of the plant that will be food for the hatched caterpillar.

Finally, it's time to fly away.

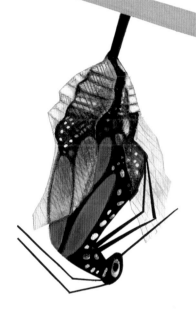

When the butterfly is fully grown, it emerges from the chrysalis.

The butterfly pumps a special fluid into its wings until they are full size.

Once its wings are dry, the butterfly must exercise them.

PARTS OF A BUTTERFLY

Like all insects, a butterfly's body is made up of three parts (a head, a thorax and an abdomen). Butterflies also have four wings, two antennae and one proboscis. And all butterflies have three pairs of legs, although in some species the front pair is small and can be hard to see.

It is common for female and male butterflies of the same species to look quite different. Males are often more colorful than females, but the differences can also include wing pattern and size.

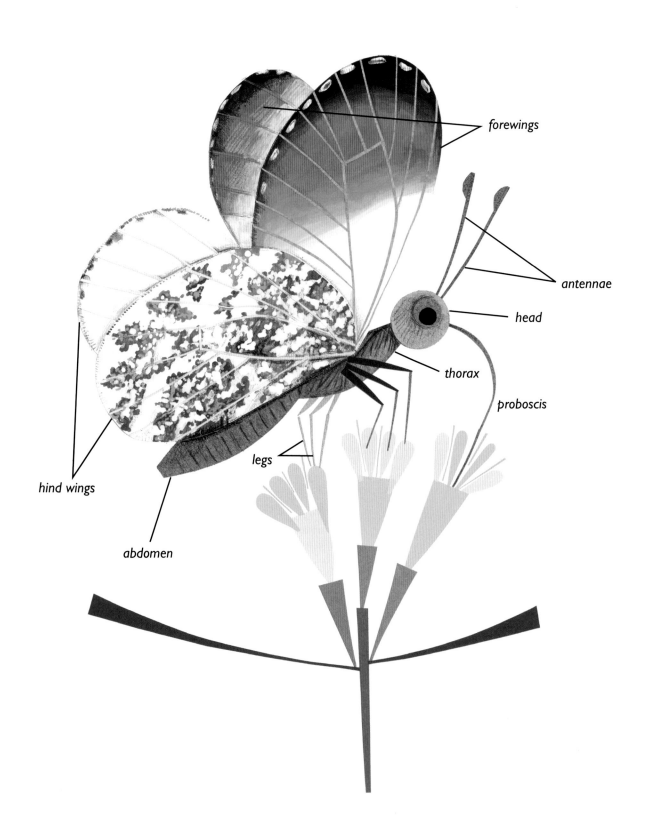

WHERE DO BUTTERFLIES LIVE?

Butterflies can be found on every continent except Antarctica! This map of the world shows you where the butterflies in this book live. And, of course, insects don't read maps so some of the butterflies in this collection can be found on more than one continent.

LEGEND

North America (pages 10 to 17)

Central and South America (pages 18 to 23)

Europe (pages 24 to 31)

Asia (pages 32 to 37)

Africa and the Middle East (pages 38 to 43)

Oceania (pages 44 to 47)

Antarctica

Monarch
Danaus plexippus

Monarchs are some of the most recognizable butterflies
in North America. But their distinct orange-and-black
markings are actually a warning to predators to *stay away*!
Monarchs have toxins in their bodies from all the milkweed
leaves they fed on as caterpillars, which makes them very
bad-tasting and even poisonous if eaten.

Monarchs are also famous for their yearly migration. They fly thousands of miles south to spend the winter in the warmer climate of central Mexico. Then, in the spring, the butterflies begin their migration back north again, stopping partway to mate and lay eggs. The butterflies hatched from these eggs are the ones that continue the journey.

Orange Sulphur
Colias eurytheme

These butterflies feed on the nectar of a number of different flowers, including dandelions, milkweeds and goldenrods.

Northern Blue
Plebejus idas

Northern Blue butterflies have a special relationship with ants. In their caterpillar stage, they make a sweet liquid that ants like to feed on. In return, the ants protect the caterpillars from predators, such as wasps and spiders.

Butterflies suck up liquid food, such as nectar, using a straw-like mouthpart called a proboscis.

Giant Swallowtail
Papilio cresphontes

As its name might suggest, the Giant Swallowtail is the largest butterfly in North America. This impressive butterfly seems to fly effortlessly, often gliding long distances between each beat of its wide wings.

The butterflies in the swallowtail family are named for the shape of their lower wings, which often look like the long tail feathers of a swallow.

Pine White
Neophasia menapia

Female Pine White butterflies lay their tiny green eggs in a delicate row on the narrow needles of coniferous trees.

Rocky Mountain Parnassian
Parnassius smintheus

These butterflies are fast flyers whose strong wings make a flapping sound as they zip through the mountain meadows where they live.

Blue Morpho
Morpho menelaus

The Blue Morpho is one of the world's largest and perhaps most beautiful butterflies. That's because we see a dazzling, shimmering blue when its wings are open. But what a difference when the Blue Morpho's wings are closed! The undersides are a much duller brown and are marked with eyespots. The drab color helps act as camouflage, and the eyespots are thought to scare off birds, a natural predator.

Snowflake
Leucidia brephos

This *tiny* white butterfly spends its life in the dark corners of the Amazon rainforest.

Malachite

Siproeta stelenes

Malachite butterflies' green wings help them stay
hidden among leafy foliage as they bask in the sun.

Cramer's Eighty-eight
Diaethria clymena

Amazingly, the black pattern on the underside of this butterfly's wings looks like the number 88 — almost like it is wearing a team jersey!

Itys Leafwing
Zaretis itys

Look closely. This dead leaf is actually the Itys Leafwing butterfly! Its wings even mimic the natural wear and tear of a real leaf.

Paradise Phantom
Cithaerias phantoma

These ghostly little butterflies have transparent wings with tips that look like they've been dipped in pink paint.

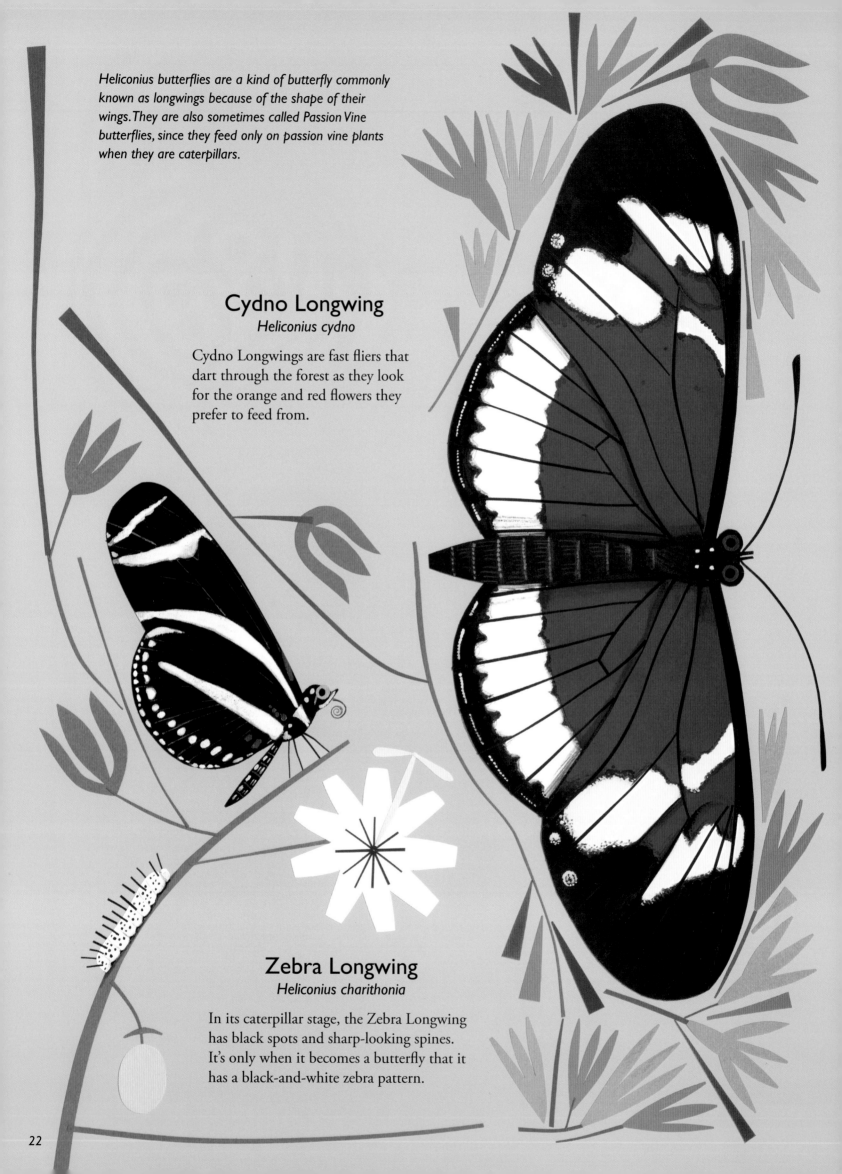

Heliconius butterflies are a kind of butterfly commonly known as longwings because of the shape of their wings. They are also sometimes called Passion Vine butterflies, since they feed only on passion vine plants when they are caterpillars.

Cydno Longwing
Heliconius cydno

Cydno Longwings are fast fliers that dart through the forest as they look for the orange and red flowers they prefer to feed from.

Zebra Longwing
Heliconius charithonia

In its caterpillar stage, the Zebra Longwing has black spots and sharp-looking spines. It's only when it becomes a butterfly that it has a black-and-white zebra pattern.

Montane Longwing
Heliconius clysonymus

Like all members of the longwing butterfly family, Montane Longwings feed on both pollen and nectar. The longwings' special diet means they tend to live longer than most other kinds of butterflies.

Tiger Longwing
Heliconius hecale

The Tiger Longwing's bold wing pattern is for attracting a mate but also for warning away predators. Toxins in the passionflower leaves that all longwing butterflies eat as caterpillars make them very unpleasant-tasting as adults.

European Peacock
Aglais io

Although there are many butterflies that live in places that have cold seasons, the European Peacock is one of the few that hibernates as an adult. These butterflies are named for the beautiful markings on their outer wings, but it is the brown underside of their wings that keeps them safely camouflaged as they hide away in buildings or hollow tree trunks over the winter. And if they happen to be discovered by mice or other small rodents, these butterflies will hiss to scare away the predator!

Purple Emperor
Apatura iris

Rather than feed on nectar or pollen from flowers, the Purple Emperor butterfly dines on sweet liquids such as tree sap and the honeydew made by aphids. The male butterflies sometimes also feed on a smellier diet of animal dung and rotting dead animals.

Red Admiral
Vanessa atalanta

Male Red Admirals fiercely defend their territory, chasing away other males and other kinds of butterflies. They are much friendlier to humans, though. Red Admiral butterflies are known to land on people, using them as perches.

Spanish Festoon
Zerynthia rumina

The intricate wing patterns of the Spanish
Festoon butterfly are very distinctive and likely
very distracting for a predator.

Green Hairstreak
Callophrys rubi

When feeding or resting on vegetation, the green undersides of this butterfly's wings blend in perfectly with the leaves of plants. The brown topsides of its wings are seen only as it flies.

Cleopatra
Gonepteryx cleopatra

Sunny in both habitat and coloring, the male Cleopatra butterfly is bright yellow with an orange patch on its forewings. This coloring can also be seen at the late stage of the chrysalis, just before the adult is ready to emerge.

Orange Tip
Anthocharis cardamines

The pale green or brownish chrysalis of the Orange Tip butterfly is curved and looks something like a tiny boomerang! Both the coloring and unusual shape help it blend in with the foliage around it.

Kaiser-i-Hind
Teinopalpus imperialis

Fast-flying Kaiser-i-Hind butterflies race
through the forest treetops in the mountain
areas where they live. Occasionally, though,
these rare butterflies stop to sun themselves
on plants on the ground below. Then they
stay completely still.

Common Windmill
Byasa polyeuctes

Common Windmill butterflies are members of the
swallowtail family. Their wide, solid-black forewings
look very different from their hind "tail" wings,
which have red-and-white markings and wavy edges.

Five-bar Swordtail
Graphium antiphates

Five-bar Swordtail butterflies are a mud-puddling type of butterfly. Mud-puddling is when butterflies (sometimes only the males) gather in groups around puddles of water, mud or even animal dung to sip up liquids that contain the salts and minerals they need.

Common Jezebel
Delias eucharis

The bright colors of the Common Jezebel tell predators that it would be a nasty-tasting meal. But it's the underside of its wings that are most colorful and eye-catching. This way, the warning is seen by birds looking up at these high-flying butterflies.

Red Pierrot
Talicada nyseus

This little butterfly prefers the shade to sun and can be seen flying late into the evening.

Dead Leaf
Kallima inachus

When its wings are open, the Dead Leaf butterfly displays a lively blue sheen with orange patches. But when its wings are closed, this butterfly looks just like a dried-up leaf, which is excellent camouflage for avoiding hungry birds looking for a juicy insect to eat.

Small Green Awlet
Burara amara

Small Green Awlet butterflies are most active during the early morning and early evening.

Sahara Swallowtail
Papilio saharae

These butterflies live in rocky and dry terrains. Sahara swallowtails are one of over 500 members of the swallowtail butterfly family.

African Queen
Danaus chrysippus

The African Queen has similar coloring to another butterfly with a royal name, the Monarch.

Polka Dot

Pardopsis punctatissima

The slow-flying Polka Dot butterfly can be easy to "spot" as it flutters through the grasslands where it lives.

Eyed Pansy
Junonia orithya

Like all butterflies, the Eyed Pansy's wings are covered in thousands of tiny scales that create the colors and patterns. The eyespot pattern on the Eyed Pansy's wings are very noticeable and likely help scare away predators.

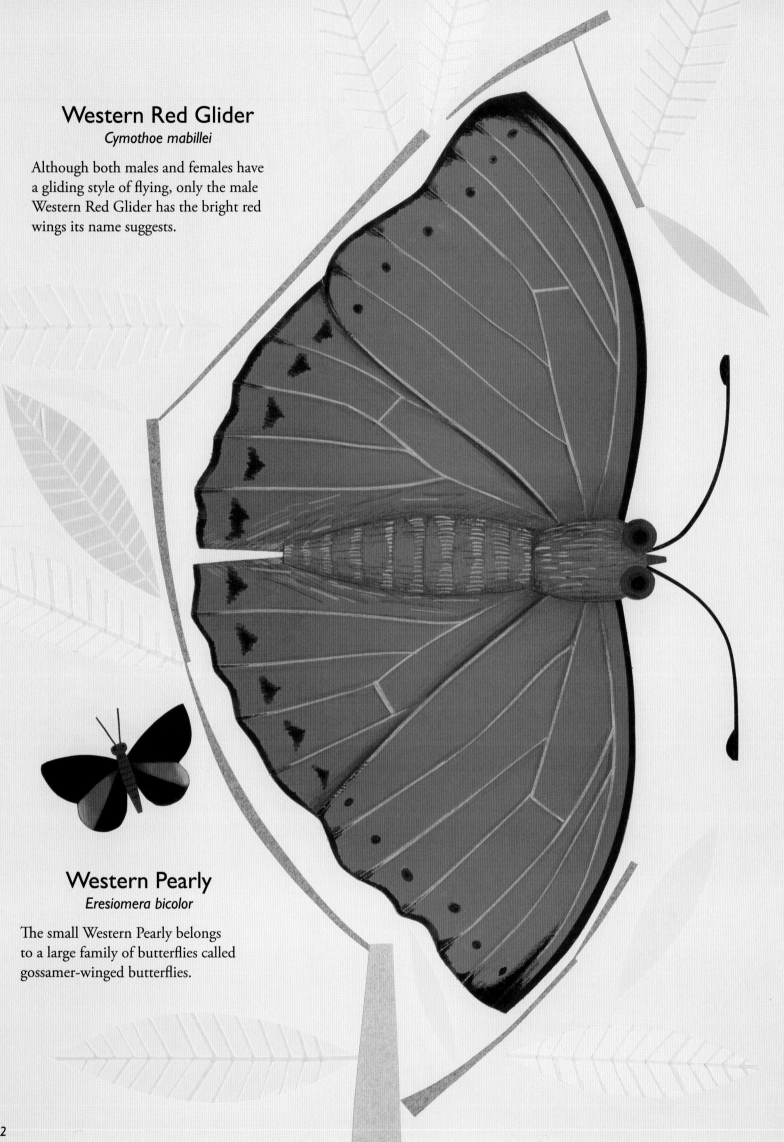

Western Red Glider
Cymothoe mabillei

Although both males and females have a gliding style of flying, only the male Western Red Glider has the bright red wings its name suggests.

Western Pearly
Eresiomera bicolor

The small Western Pearly belongs to a large family of butterflies called gossamer-winged butterflies.

Janetta Themis Forester
Euphaedra janetta

Janetta Themis Forester butterflies are low flyers, fluttering along the rainforest floor in search of the fallen fruit they feed on.

Queen Alexandra's Birdwing
Ornithoptera alexandrae

The Queen Alexandra's Birdwing is the largest butterfly in the world. The female's wingspan can be up to 30 cm (12 in), which is about as wide as a dinner plate! The males are about half this size, but are more brightly colored. Despite its spectacular size, the butterfly is rarely seen and can only be found in one small coastal rainforest in Papua New Guinea. And unfortunately, the Queen Alexandra's Birdwing is now endangered because its habitat is being destroyed.

Small Pearl White
Elodina walkeri

The Small Pearl White is much smaller than the Queen Alexandra's Birdwing butterfly but a bit larger than the Tiny Grass Blue.

Tiny Grass Blue
Zizula hylax

The Tiny Grass Blue is one of
the smallest butterflies in the
world. Its wingspan is about the
width of a dime.

Great Eggfly
Hypolimnas bolina

The female Great Eggfly is unusually doting for a butterfly parent.
After laying her clutch of eggs on the underside of a carefully
chosen leaf, she is known to stay and guard against predators.

Common Brown

Heteronympha merope

Common Brown butterflies usually fly slowly — until they sense a threat, such as a nearby bird. Then they move in a quick zigzagging pattern as they try to confuse the predator and make a getaway.

GLOSSARY

camouflage – the markings and coloring that allow butterflies to blend in with their surroundings and to hide from predators.

clutch – a group of eggs laid at one time.

coniferous – a type of tree or shrub that has cones containing its seeds, and leaves that are usually thin and needle-like.

habitat – an area where a particular species of butterfly lives. A mountain meadow is an example of a habitat.

host plant – a plant used for food by butterflies and caterpillars. Butterflies always lay their eggs on a host plant.

mud-puddling – when groups of butterflies (sometimes only the males) gather around puddles to sip up liquids that contain salts and minerals.

predator – an animal that hunts and eats other animals to survive.

proboscis – the straw-like mouthpart a butterfly uses when feeding on liquids.

wingspan – the measurement of a butterfly from wingtip to wingtip.

FOR MORE INFORMATION

Here are some of the invaluable sources I used to create this book. Through my research, I learned so much about butterflies and the different plants they need to thrive and survive, many of which are found in ecosystems that are at risk from pollution and destructive building practices. The more we know about Earth's creatures, the more we understand our role in protecting them and their habitats.

BOOKS

1,000 Butterflies: An Illustrated Guide to the World's Most Beautiful Butterflies by Adrian Hoskins, New Holland Publishers, 2016.

Butterflies of the World by Adrian Hoskins, New Holland Publishers, 2015.

Butterflies of the World by Gilles Martin and Myriam Baran, Abrams, 2006.

Kaufman Field Guide to Butterflies of North America by Jim P. Brock and Kenn Kaufman, Houghton Mifflin Harcourt, 2006.

National Audubon Society Field Guide to Butterflies: North America by Robert Michael Pyle, Knopf Publishing Group, 1981.

Weird Butterflies & Moths by Ronald Orenstein and Thomas Marent, Firefly, 2016.

WEBSITES

Butterfly Conservation butterfly-conservation.org

Cambridge Butterfly Conservatory cambridgebutterfly.com

Learn About Butterflies: The Complete Guide to the World of Butterflies and Moths learnaboutbutterflies.com

BOOKS OF INTEREST TO YOUNG READERS

Butterflies and Moths by David Carter, Eyewitness Handbooks, Dorling Kindersley, 1992.

Butterflies & Moths by John Farndon, Exploring Nature series, Armadillo Books, 2015.

Butterfly & Moth by Paul Whalley, Eyewitness Books, Knopf Books for Young Readers, 1988.

Butterflies Belong Here: A Story of One Idea, Thirty Kids, and a World of Butterflies by Deborah Hopkinson, illustrated by Meilo So, Chronicle Books, 2020.

A Children's Guide to Arctic Butterflies by Mia Pelletier, illustrated by Danny Christopher, Inhabit Media, 2019.

The Girl Who Drew Butterflies: How Maria Merian's Art Changed Science by Joyce Sidman, HMH Books for Young Readers, 2018.

How to Be a Butterfly by Laura Knowles, illustrated by Catell Ronca, words & pictures, 2019.

Waiting for Wings by Lois Ehlert, HMH Books for Young Readers, 2001.

INDEX

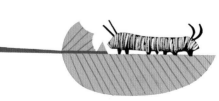

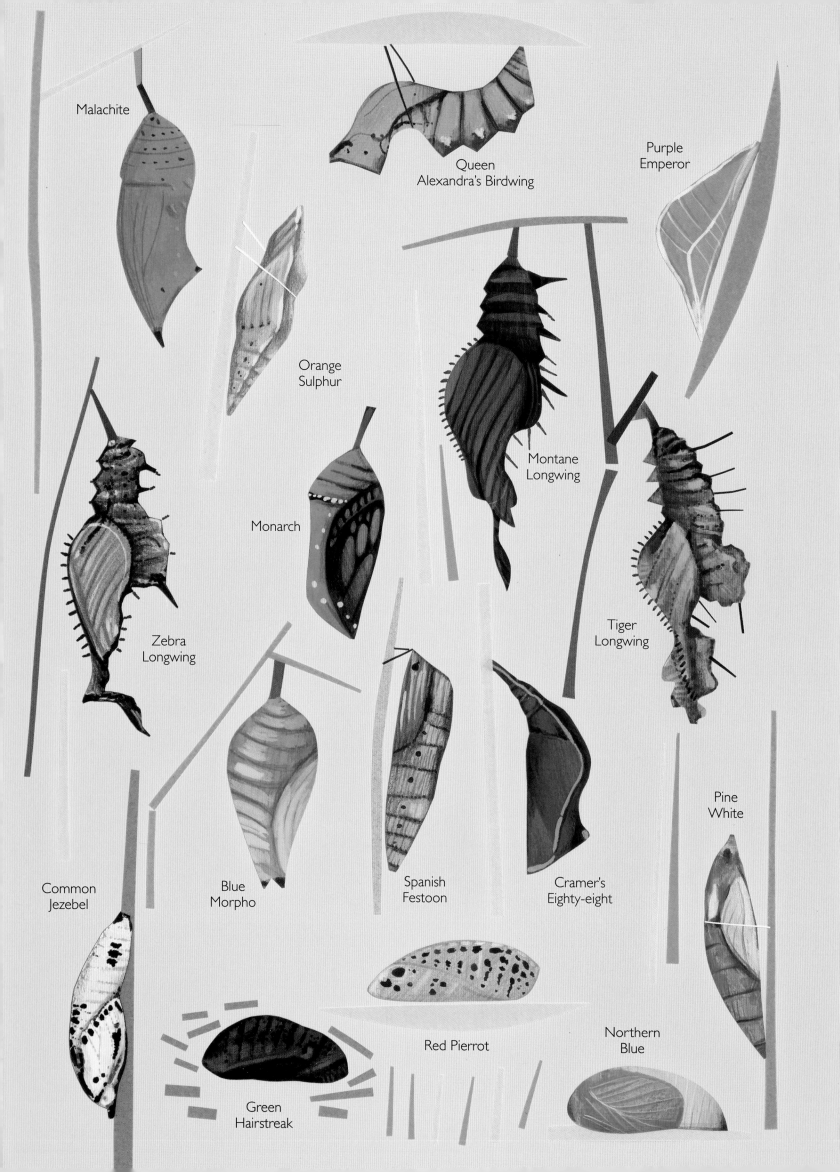

Malachite

Queen
Alexandra's Birdwing

Purple
Emperor

Orange
Sulphur

Montane
Longwing

Monarch

Zebra
Longwing

Tiger
Longwing

Pine
White

Common
Jezebel

Blue
Morpho

Spanish
Festoon

Cramer's
Eighty-eight

Green
Hairstreak

Red Pierrot

Northern
Blue